THRILLER OF
THE YEAR

by

GLYN JONES

SAMUEL   FRENCH

LONDON

NEW YORK TORONTO SYDNEY HOLLYWOOD

© 1968 by Glyn Jones

ISBN 0 573 03016 2

THRILLER OF THE YEAR

First produced on 31st July 1967 at Golders Green Hippodrome with the following cast of characters:

(in order of their appearance)

GILLIAN HOWARD (a thriller writer)   *Heather Chasen*
IRENE KNIGHT (her publisher)   *Elizabeth Weaver*
MADGE ROBINSON (her secretary)   *Kathleen Moffatt*
BERYL SPENCE (her doctor)   *Judith Harte*
EDITH HOWARD (her mother-in-law)   *Gabrielle Hamilton*

The voices of:
> PETRA TRACEY (Gillian's agent)
> CONRAD KNIGHT (Irene's husband)
> MARTIN HOWARD (Gillian's husband)

The Play directed by BEN HAWTHORNE
Setting by SUSAN AYERS

SYNOPSIS OF SCENES

The action of the play takes place in the lounge of Gillian Howard's London flat

ACT I

Evening

ACT II

Half an hour later

ACT III

Twenty minutes later

Time—the present

ACT I

SCENE—*The lounge of Gillian Howard's flat in London. A night in winter. The decoration and furniture in the room, a mixture of antique and contemporary, befits a woman of elegance and taste, and one who has the means of indulging that taste. The entrance to the lounge is through a wide, foyer-like hall up* R, *the door of which leads to the outside corridor of the block of flats. There is a door to the kitchen down* L *of the Lounge, and up* L *of the hall another door leads to the bedroom and the rest of the apartment.*

When the CURTAIN *rises, the flat is in darkness. It is late on a cold, wet, windy, miserable winter's night. There is the sound of lift gates opening. A moment later the front door is flung open to reveal* GILLIAN HOWARD *in a shaft of light from the corridor. She flicks on the lights and storms into the flat leaving the door open. Realizing she is alone, she turns back to the door as she takes off her coat.*

GILLIAN. Home. Safe and sound. All in one piece. Satisfied? Or do you actually want to see me tucked up in bed?

(IRENE KNIGHT *appears at the front door*)

IRENE. I thought a night-cap might be in order.
GILLIAN. It isn't.
IRENE. And I want to talk to you.
GILLIAN. Can't it—Oh, come in if you must.
IRENE. Thank you.

(IRENE *steps into the hall and closes the door behind her.* GILLIAN *flings down her coat on the chair in the hall, and moves into the lounge*)

GILLIAN. Tell me, Irene, do you watch so solicitously over all your writers?
IRENE (*removing her coat and hanging it in the hall*) Only the more successful ones, Gillian, like you.
GILLIAN (*moving up* C) Why don't you employ a private detective?
IRENE. Maybe I have.

(GILLIAN *freezes as* IRENE *comes into the room to join her, then she forces a laugh and looks around for an escape*)

Gillian . . .
GILLIAN. Oh, God! Look at that. She's left the windows open. (*She crosses to the windows to close them and waves an airy hand towards the tray of drinks*) What about that night-cap? It might get the winter out of our bones. (*She draws the curtains*)
IRENE (*moving* LC) Might it? In that case I would have thought

you'd had enough tonight to make for the most glorious, golden, high summer on record.

GILLIAN. It was supposed to be a celebration. I was the guest of honour. My book was voted the "Thriller of the Year". The whole thing was a ghastly bore and mine's a brandy.

IRENE. As if I didn't know.

GILLIAN. Pity Conrad couldn't make it tonight. What's he doing in Rome anyway?

IRENE. What the Romans are doing, I should think.

GILLIAN. Any particular Romans?

IRENE. You know my husband.

GILLIAN. Yes.

IRENE. Just how well do you know my husband, Gillian?

GILLIAN (*moving below Irene to the L end of the couch*) What about that drink?

IRENE. Don't you think you've had enough?

GILLIAN. You mean, you think I've had enough.

(*The telephone rings.* GILLIAN *lifts the receiver, holds it for a beat of two, and replaces it*)

IRENE. You should have arranged for your calls to be transferred.

GILLIAN. Didn't think of it. I can't think of everything. I pay Madge to think for me; why doesn't she?

IRENE. She does. So successfully you don't even notice it, let alone thank her for it.

GILLIAN (*moving up L*) Is that so? Well, take a look at that. (*She picks up a handful of mail, including a package, from her working desk*) Paying Madge to take care of my personal affairs also includes the post. She hasn't even bothered to open it.

IRENE. Where is she?

GILLIAN. Away for the week-end. Don't ask me where. I shudder to think. Playing with a potter's wheel or keeping an all-night vigil on Stonehenge.

IRENE. Perhaps she has a boy-friend.

GILLIAN. Perhaps the earth is flat and the moon is made of green cheese.

IRENE. You should have invited her tonight, Gillian.

GILLIAN. Oh? Why?

IRENE. It would have been a nice gesture. Isn't it time you learnt the art of the gracious gesture? Considering what a "phenomenal" success you are.

GILLIAN. It is precisely because I am such a "phenomenal" success that I have no need to make the gracious gesture. (*She drops the post and looks out of the window*) God, this weather! (*She shudders and turns away to cross over to the electric fire*) "In this world", said Benjamin Franklin, "nothing is certain except death and taxes". Had he been an Englishman he would have added, and rain. Though which is most with us, the taxes or the rain, I really don't know.

IRENE. Or death?

GILLIAN. Or death. (*She takes up the plug*) I don't know why that girl is always pulling plugs out. She has a horror of electricity. I break my back constantly . . .

(GILLIAN *pushes home the plug. There is a bang and a flash and* GILLIAN *leaps with fright, as does* IRENE)

IRENE. Gillian! Are you all right?

GILLIAN (*waggling her fingers*) Phew! Now why did it do that?

IRENE. Must have shorted, I suppose. Not that I know much about it. Did you get a shock?

GILLIAN. Of course I got a shock. I got a shock! Well, no fire. Shhh—oooh—I hope it hasn't blown a fuse. Now I really could do with a drink. What's it to be? (*She moves above the couch*)

IRENE. Coffee.

GILLIAN. Coffee?

IRENE. Yes, please. With *hot* milk.

GILLIAN. Considering it is your success as much as mine—financially that is—coffee hardly seems the appropriate beverage with which to celebrate. However, if you want coffee, coffee it shall be. I hope it keeps you awake all night.

IRENE. The only thing that ever keeps me awake is an uneasy conscience. Does it do that to you?

GILLIAN. I don't really know. Never having had one.

IRENE. Well, something's eating you.

GILLIAN. I'm tired. I need a holiday.

IRENE. What? You've had three this year.

GILLIAN. Then I need another. Only this time I leave everything behind me, including the typewriter. Go away, forget it all, and don't tell anyone where I'm going.

(*The telephone rings.* GILLIAN *moves above the table, lifts the receiver, holds it, then puts it down*)

You see? It never stops.

IRENE. How do you know that isn't an offer for the film rights?

GILLIAN. It's one o'clock in the morning.

IRENE. Breakfast-time in Hollywood.

GILLIAN. If anyone was going to make an offer for the film rights, they would have done so by now. And, if anyone is doing it now, then you and Petra can deal with it at your respective offices and not bother me. Next time the phone rings I leave it off the hook. It's a menace.

(GILLIAN *returns to the desk, where she unwraps the package that is with the post*)

IRENE (*moving up* C) You're not very grateful for man's ingenuity, are you?

GILLIAN. Ingenious men are hard to come by.

IRENE. Is that why you've taken to poaching?

GILLIAN. The only thing I poach, Irene, are eggs, and that I do very badly.

IRENE. Gillian Howard doesn't do anything very badly.

GILLIAN. Why, thank you. I do hope you're not going to stay long, Irene. I am very tired.

IRENE (*moving above the table* C) So am I, darling, and I do know when I'm not wanted. I shall have my cup of henbane, mount my broomstick, and fly—after we have had our little *tête-à-tête*.

(*The telephone rings. Both women turn to look at it.* GILLIAN *is about to move when* IRENE's *hand drops on to the receiver and stays there.* GILLIAN *watches her*)

Shall I answer it?

GILLIAN. Lift it up and put it down.

(*A second passes, and then* IRENE *does so*)

IRENE. Just think, if the telephone hadn't been invented the human race would have been denied a success like "Dial M For Murder". Nor would we have had a success like "The Lady Is Dead". Gillian Howard would not have written the thriller of the year and be the wealthy woman she is. Conrad and I would not be the successful publishers we are. And Petra would not be the wealthy agent she is. So God bless the telephone and so say all of us.

GILLIAN. God bless Gillian Howard seems more to the point.

IRENE. Perhaps he does, dear—only we don't notice.

GILLIAN (*moving* L *of Irene with the package*) Look at this—a copy of "The Lady Is Dead". Now, why should anyone want to send me a copy of my own book?

IRENE. To be autographed?

GILLIAN. No—there's no letter—nothing—just the book.

IRENE. No criticism?

(GILLIAN *gives Irene a sharp look*)

Well, while you're pondering over the mystery I'll put on the milk. Otherwise I'll never get that cup of coffee and I'm dying for it. (*She moves down* L *to the kitchen*)

GILLIAN. Irene—why should anyone send me a copy of my own book? I don't get it.

IRENE. You're the successful writer of thrillers, dear. The puzzle is there to be solved, solve it. Be your own detective.

(IRENE *exits into the kitchen*)

GILLIAN (*moving above the couch*) Very funny. (*She lights a cigarette from the box on the table and looks at the book, flicking through it*) Who? Who? And why?

IRENE (*off*) I can't find the coffee. Where do you keep it?
GILLIAN. In the spin-dryer next to the cornflakes.
IRENE (*off*) What?
GILLIAN. Oh, never mind. I'll do it.

(IRENE *appears at the kitchen door and* GILLIAN *tosses the book to her as she crosses to go into the kitchen*)

IRENE. Such a gracious lady—so sweet—so charming in manner.

(IRENE *moves back into the room and puts the book on the couch, as the front door opens and* MADGE *enters. She closes the door and starts to take off her coat*)

Madge!
MADGE (*moving* C *to* R *of Irene*) Oh, hello, Mrs Knight. I didn't expect—where's Mrs Howard?

(IRENE *points to the kitchen*)

Someone left the lift gates open again. I had to walk up. It's so thoughtless of people. (*She hangs her coat on the hooks*)
IRENE. Oh dear. We are the thoughtless ones.
MADGE. Oh—I didn't mean . . .
IRENE (*raising a hand to stop her*) No. It's no fun walking up four flights of stairs. I apologize.
MADGE. Oh, people are always forgetting.
IRENE. Anyway, I thought you were away for the week-end.
MADGE. I was. The arrangements were cancelled, unfortunately.
IRENE. Welcome back to the jungle. It hasn't changed much since you've been away. Is it still raining?
MADGE. Worse than ever. Thank heavens I took my umbrella.

(*There is a loud explosion from the kitchen.* IRENE *and* MADGE *stand absolutely motionless, looking towards the kitchen, seemingly too stunned to move.* GILLIAN *appears at the door. She is badly shaken*)

IRENE. Gillian! What happened?

(GILLIAN *staggers into the room and collapses on the couch with* IRENE *hovering in front of her.* MADGE *pauses in the doorway and then dashes into the kitchen.* IRENE *looks desperately around the room, sees the drinks on the tray and, with shaky hands, starts to pour a brandy as* MADGE *reappears at the kitchen door*)

Is brandy good for shock?
MADGE. I don't know. I think so.

(IRENE *nods and takes the glass over to Gillian*)

IRENE. Here, Gillian—drink this. Come on, drink it.

(IRENE *holds the glass to Gillian's mouth, but* GILLIAN, *still in a state of shock, moves her head away, rather like a child avoiding nasty medicine, and knocks the glass flying. She stares with wide, terrified eyes at Irene)*

Gillian! It's all right. It's me, Irene. Gillian! Madge, who's her doctor?

MADGE. Spence.

IRENE. Get him.

    (MADGE *picks up an address book from the desk and finds the number while* IRENE *lifts* GILLIAN *from the couch)*

Come on, Gillian—into the bedroom and lie down.

GILLIAN. No—no, I'm all right now.

IRENE. Don't argue. Come along, into the bedroom and lie down.

    (MADGE *moves to the phone, but before she can lift it it starts to ring.* IRENE *pauses up* RC *in leading Gillian from the room)*

Take it off and put it down again.

MADGE. What?

IRENE. Take it off and put it down. Disengage it, girl, and then get the doctor; this is an emergency.

    (IRENE *hurries back, lifts the phone, puts it down and then goes back to Gillian and into the bedroom as* MADGE *starts to dial. We hear the phone ring at the other end and then a sleepy woman's voice answer. This is* DOCTOR SPENCE)

SPENCE (*on the phone*) Doctor Spence.

MADGE. Oh doctor, Madge Robinson here, Mrs Howard's secretary.

SPENCE. Yes, Madge?

MADGE. Can you come over straight away? There's been an accident.

SPENCE. What accident?

MADGE. A gas explosion. No one hurt or anything, but Mrs Howard seems badly shaken. She's being put to bed, but I think . . .

SPENCE. I'll be right over.

    (*The phone clicks off at the other end*)

MADGE. Thank you. (*She puts down the phone, picks up the glass and goes to put it on the tray*)

    (IRENE *enters*)

IRENE. Did you get the doctor?

MADGE. Yes. She's coming straight over.

    (MADGE *makes for the bedroom door, but* IRENE *stops her*)

IRENE. Leave her alone, Madge. Don't make a fuss. You know what she's like.

MADGE. How is she?

IRENE. She'll be all right. Just leave her alone.

(MADGE *turns back, picks up the tray, and starts for the kitchen*)

Where are you going with that?

MADGE. To the kitchen.

IRENE. You're not, you know. After all that I need a drink. To hell with coffee. (*She moves to the fire*)

MADGE. Well—Mrs Howard isn't really supposed to take alcohol and I didn't want it to be around when Doctor Spence arrives.

IRENE. Surely she can keep some in the flat for guests?

MADGE. Yes but—well—out of sight, out of mind.

IRENE (*laughing*) What? For someone who's not supposed to drink she certainly had a skinful tonight. The good doctor's going to know anyway, so come on—(*She waves an imperious hand*)—give me a medicinal brandy before I pass out.

MADGE. I really think I . . .

IRENE. Don't argue, Madge! Don't argue. Or I'll be the next one to pass out and the good doctor will have two to cope with.

MADGE. If not three.

IRENE. Come off it, Madge. You're made of much sterner stuff.

MADGE. On the contrary, Mrs Knight.

IRENE. You must be. To have stuck it out with her all these years. I must admit I find it all a bit Victorian, this mistress servant set-up.

MADGE. I really think I ought to look in and . . .

IRENE. Worry about me, Madge. It will make a nice change.

(MADGE *replaces the tray and starts to pour the drink*)

Did I hear you say the doctor is a she?

MADGE. That's right.

IRENE (*sitting on the couch*) Funny, never thought of Gillian having a woman doctor. Of course, I've heard her talking about Doctor—what's her name?

MADGE. Spence, Beryl Spence.

IRENE. But I've always imagined it to be a man. I suppose that is because of Gillian.

MADGE. Mrs Howard is a great believer in the old saying that work and pleasure never mix.

IRENE. Is she now?

MADGE (*moving L of the couch and handing Irene her drink*) If you don't encounter temptation, you don't have to go through all the bother of resisting it. Most of her business associates are women.

IRENE. Most—but not all. My husband, for instance? An exception to prove the rule, no doubt. Is the good doctor married?

MADGE. No.

IRENE. Lucky old her. Aren't you drinking?

(MADGE *shakes her head*)

Don't you drink?

(MADGE *shakes her head*)

Never?

MADGE. Hardly. Certainly not spirits.

IRENE. You're not afraid some nasty man might get you under the weather and play havoc with your morality.

MADGE. You need have no fear for my morality, Mrs Knight.

IRENE. That makes a nice change around here.

MADGE. What has Mrs Howard said to you about me?

IRENE. What should she have said?

MADGE. Judging by your attitude, nothing complimentary.

IRENE. My attitude? Madge, you really shouldn't be quite so touchy.

MADGE. I think I have a right to be.

IRENE. Why stay with her, then?

MADGE. Oh, I don't know—any number of reasons—security— maybe it's just a habit.

IRENE. Yes, and bad habits are the hardest to kick. But take heart, Madge. You are not the only one. What about her husband, Martin? She eventually kicked him out. Though not completely, you'll notice.

MADGE. Mrs Knight, don't you think we should let him know? About the accident?

IRENE. Why?

MADGE. I just thought.

IRENE (*waving towards the phone*) Go ahead. Though, unless she were at death's door, I doubt whether you would arouse much interest. How long will it take for that doctor to get here? I'm tired. All I want now is to get home and into bed.

MADGE. She shouldn't be long. She hasn't far to come.

IRENE. Well, as soon as she's been and done her stuff, I'm off. In the meantime I think I'll have another night-cap. You wouldn't like to do the honours, I suppose?

(IRENE *holds out her glass.* MADGE *takes it and goes back to the bottle of brandy*)

Is it my imagination or is there one hell of a draught blowing through here?

MADGE. I left the kitchen window open. (*She moves towards the kitchen*)

IRENE. Leave it. Did you fix whatever it was in there?

MADGE. I think there's a gas leak somewhere around the stove. I turned it off at the main.

(*The phone rings.* IRENE *reacts, but* MADGE *moves over to it*)

I'll get it. (*She lifts the receiver*) Knightsbridge four three . . .

(PETRA'S *voice is heard in the receiver*)

PETRA (*on the phone*) Is that you, Madge?

MADGE. Yes.

PETRA. It's Petra Tracey. Is Gillian there?

MADGE. One moment, Miss Tracey. (*She covers the mouthpiece with her hand*) It's her agent.

IRENE (*rising*) Give.

(IRENE *takes the phone and clicks her fingers at Madge for her drink.* MADGE *gives Irene the glass, then takes the tray and exits into the kitchen*)

Petra.

PETRA. Who's that?

IRENE. It's Irene.

PETRA. Irene! How did it go?

IRENE. Wonderful, darling. Book yourself a Caribbean cruise.

PETRA. Oh, I am sorry I couldn't make it. Is Gillian there? I want to congratulate her.

IRENE. Of course you do, dear. But, unfortunately, you can't, not at the moment. There's been a little accident.

PETRA. What?

IRENE. Don't get excited, dear. Your percentage is quite safe, I think. No, you see she blew herself up with the gas stove.

PETRA. What!

IRENE. She singed the feathers on her arms, dear, that's all. I always said she needed electrolysis. (*She glances at the fire*) Come to think of it, she nearly got that tonight, too.

PETRA. Don't be a bitch.

IRENE. Oh, darling, you know me. It's my way of coping with a crisis.

PETRA. Are you sure she's all right, Irene? Shall I come over?

IRENE. No, I wouldn't do that, dear. The smell of sulphur and brimstone is something alarming. And we're just waiting on the doctor, so there is nothing else we can do.

(*The front doorbell rings*)

And I do declare she has arrived.

(MADGE *enters from the kitchen and crosses up* R *to open the door*)

MADGE. Doctor.

IRENE. Give me a call in the morning, Petra. Not too early. Good night.

(IRENE *puts down the phone and turns as* MADGE *admits* DOCTOR SPENCE *who passes straight through the room and out to the bedroom, glancing at Irene in passing, but no more*)

Good evening. Well . . .

(MADGE *dithers for a moment by the door and then follows the doctor, closing the door behind her.* IRENE *gulps down her drink*)

That's what I like about these dedicated, professional women, so charming. (*She goes to pour herself another drink only to find the tray has disappeared*) Now, what has she . . . (*She marches into the kitchen, to return carrying the bottle and pouring herself another drink*) This is becoming too much of a good thing, Irene Knight. (*She moves to the table above the couch*)

> (*The telephone rings.* IRENE *puts down the bottle with a bang and stares at the instrument. She glances towards the far doors and then hurries across to the phone to answer it. The* OPERATOR's *voice is heard*)

Yes?

OPERATOR (*on the phone*) Five-eight-four-one-two-three-nine?

IRENE. Yes.

OPERATOR. Mr Knight is making a person to person call from Rome, can Mrs Gillian Howard take the call, please?

IRENE. This is Gillian Howard speaking.

OPERATOR. Hold the line, please.

> (IRENE *glances anxiously towards the doors*)

You're through now.

> (CONRAD's *voice is heard on the phone*)

CONRAD (*on the phone*) Hello, Gillian?

IRENE. Yes.

CONRAD. Oh, thank God. I've been so worried, darling. What on earth's the matter with your phone?

IRENE. We were cut off.

CONRAD. You can say that again. Darling? Can you hear me?

IRENE. Yes, I can hear you—loud and clear.

CONRAD. Well, I can hardly hear you. (*After a pause*) There's nothing wrong, is there?

IRENE. No.

CONRAD. You sound strange.

IRENE. Why are you phoning?

CONRAD. Gillian, there *is* something the matter. How did it go tonight?

IRENE. All right.

CONRAD. That's not very enthusiastic. I miss you. What you need is a holiday. Why don't you take a few days off and join me here?

IRENE. You wouldn't like that.

CONRAD. What? Do speak up, darling.

IRENE. I can't. Conrad, I must ring off now. Irene is here. Don't phone again tonight.

CONRAD. What?

SPENCE (*off*) Thank you, Madge. I can cope now.

IRENE (*glancing quickly towards the door*) I must go.

CONRAD. Gill!

(IRENE *puts down the phone*)

IRENE. I *was* right.

(MADGE *enters. She notices the bottle of brandy and frowns*)

And how is everything in the sick-room?
MADGE (*moving down* C) I think she will be all right now.
IRENE. I'm so glad.

(IRENE *gulps down the rest of her drink.* MADGE *watches her*)

We wouldn't want the goose to pop off without laying another golden egg, would we? Well, home, James, and don't spare the horses.

(IRENE *puts the glass on the table and goes to the hall for her coat.* MADGE *gathers up the glass and bottle and takes them into the kitchen.* IRENE *turns around*)

If there's anything I can do, Madge . . . Now where the hell has she got to? Madge?

(*The telephone rings*)

I'll get it! (*She goes over to the phone and lifts the receiver, holds it a second, puts it back*) We really can't be doing with that (*She takes off the receiver and leaves it off*)

(DOCTOR SPENCE *enters and stands by the door up* RC. IRENE *sees her, and moves upstage to her*)

Doctor Spence—I'm Irene Knight, Mrs Howard's publisher. How do you do? (*She holds out her hand*)
SPENCE. How do you do.

(*They shake hands*)

IRENE. I'm so sorry we had to call you out of your warm bed, but these things do have a habit of happening, don't they? I mean, gas stoves blowing up in the middle of the night. Well, it was either you or the fire brigade. Hmn. How is the patient, anyway?
SPENCE. She's fine. (*She puts her bag on the chair in the hall*)
IRENE. Oh. It was one of those unnecessary calls, then. I am sorry.
SPENCE. Not at all. She naturally received quite a shock.
IRENE. Well, that's all right then. As long as you haven't been inconvenienced.
SPENCE. If there is genuine cause for concern I am never inconvenienced.
IRENE. Good. Then at least have a drink before you go.
SPENCE. Thank you. Scotch.
IRENE. Scotch. (*She starts towards the kitchen*) Madge, bless her heart, thought you would be terribly disapproving if you found the

room littered with bottles. She carted them all off to the kitchen. Madge? The good doctor would like a Scotch. (*To Spence*) How?

SPENCE. Water, half and half.

IRENE (*calling to Madge*) Water, half and half. (*She turns back to Spence and smiles sweetly*)

SPENCE. I thought Madge was away for the week-end.

IRENE. Cancelled. I didn't ask why. Thought it might be indelicate.

SPENCE. It's just as well Mrs Howard has someone with her.

IRENE. Isn't it?

SPENCE. I wish she'd take things a little easier. She works much too hard. How did the big occasion go this evening?

IRENE. Big.

(MADGE *enters with the drink and moves to* L *of Spence*)

SPENCE (*taking the drink*) Ah, thank you, Madge. (*To Irene*) Aren't you having one?

(MADGE *moves above Irene to the door* L)

IRENE. Hmn—I really think I've had quite enough for one evening.

SPENCE. Yes, so has Gillian, expressly against my orders.

IRENE. I might just manage another, though. (*She looks at Madge*)

(MADGE *obediently exits* L *for the drink*)

SPENCE. I've warned Gillian about overindulging. She has a slight heart condition which makes it unwise.

IRENE. Oh? I didn't know that.

SPENCE. Why should you?

IRENE. Girl talk.

SPENCE (*moving to the fire*) Being the kind of woman she is, Gillian would hardly go around shouting it from the rooftops.

IRENE. And being the kind of woman I am, I am not in the habit of being shouted at from rooftops.

(MADGE *enters with the drink*)

But the gas going up nearly gave me heart failure. And I'm sure it nearly gave Madge heart failure. So how come it didn't kill her off? (*She takes the glass from Madge and moves above the table* C)

SPENCE. It could quite easily have done so.

IRENE. Then we, her devoted friends, and umpteen million devoted readers must consider ourselves very lucky.

SPENCE. I do. I don't like losing my patients—it upsets me, even when inevitable, and I'm sure you don't like losing valuable clients. Should that phone be off the hook?

IRENE. Providing no one sneaks to the Postmaster-General, I don't see why not. Blasted thing's a nuisance. It's been ringing incessantly all evening.

MADGE. One call is hardly incessant.

IRENE. There were any number before you arrived, I have no doubt there will be any number from now on. However—(*She puts the phone back on the hook*)—satisfied?

(*The phone immediately rings. Before* MADGE *can move,* IRENE *picks it up and drops it back on the cradle*)

MADGE. Why did you do that?

IRENE. It seemed such a sensible thing to do. And we learn from example.

MADGE. It might have been a very important call.

IRENE. It might.

SPENCE (*finishing her drink*) Well . . . I'll take a last look at the patient, then I'll be off. (*She moves above the couch, puts her glass on the table, and sees the book. Picking it up*) Oh, is this the masterpiece?

IRENE. You mean you haven't read it yet?

(MADGE *moves down* L)

SPENCE. A doctor's life—need I tell you—is an extremely busy one. I'll get around to it.

IRENE. If you can't get around to the public library, the retail price is sixteen shillings.

SPENCE. You mean I don't get a free autographed copy?

IRENE (*moving* LC) Even I don't get a free autographed copy.

(SPENCE *flicks open the book. Her expression changes as she starts to read*)

SPENCE (*reading*) "Still wondering about the contents of the package, Janet went through into the kitchen. Her heart missed a beat as she switched on the light. She could have sworn she saw a movement outside the door. Was there someone out there? Or was it just her overwrought imagination? Oh, why hadn't Robbie phoned? Something must be wrong. She hated these trips that took him abroad, so far from her. . . " God in heaven! Why do people read this stuff?

IRENE. It's highly gratifying that they do, otherwise I might be out of business.

(GILLIAN *enters unseen by the others and stands by the door*)

SPENCE (*reading*) "Still uneasy, and knowing someone might be on the fire escape watching her every move, Janet placed a saucepan of milk on the stove and turned on the gas. There was a blinding flash. . . " (*She stops and looks at the others. There is a silence*) Quite a coincidence.

(*There is an awkward pause, then* SPENCE *puts down the book and turns to go into the bedroom*)

IRENE. Gillian!

SPENCE. What do you think you're doing?

(GILLIAN *wanders into the room down* C, *looking around a little vacantly*)

GILLIAN. I'm feeling better.
IRENE. Well, you certainly don't look it.
MADGE. Mrs Howard, do you think you should?
GILLIAN (*snapping*) I am not a babe in arms.
SPENCE. No. You're a grown woman and you ought to have more sense. Go back to bed.
GILLIAN. I don't want to. Madge, get me a drink, will you?
SPENCE. No.
GILLIAN. I feel like a brandy.
SPENCE. I said, no.
GILLIAN. Madge?
SPENCE. I forbid it.
GILLIAN. Madge, will you stop standing there like an idiot and fetch me a good stiff brandy?
SPENCE (*moving down* R *to the fire*) I warn you, Gillian, if you disobey me I will not be responsible for the consequences.

(*There is a silence as* GILLIAN *glares from Spence to Madge. Then she gives in and turns on Irene*)

GILLIAN. I thought you would have gone by now.
IRENE. And leave you alone on your bed of suffering?
GILLIAN. You weren't thinking of joining me, I hope. I heard the phone ring. Did anyone answer it?
IRENE. No. Why? Were you expecting someone?
GILLIAN. I thought you were away for the week-end.
IRENE. Oh, no! Let's not go into that again.
SPENCE. Gillian, if you refuse to go back to bed, at least sit down, try to relax, and stop attacking everyone.

(GILLIAN *flops into the armchair* C *and covers her face with her hand. The other three look at her, their faces expressionless.* IRENE *looks from one to the other and then back to Gillian*)

IRENE. You know, Gillian, I think maybe you were right. I think maybe you should take that holiday after all.
SPENCE. Holiday? The very thing.
IRENE. A long holiday, far away from it all.
GILLIAN. What does that mean?
SPENCE. One has to admit that, in your particular case, crime has paid, handsomely in fact, but I think, maybe now, it's your turn to pay up.
GILLIAN. And what does that mean?
SPENCE. I'm talking about the strain, Gillian. The strain of living with crime, thinking crime, working on crime for so long. You've been overworking.

IRENE. The chickens are coming home to roost. It's been playing on your nerves, dear.

SPENCE. That's why you're so edgy.

GILLIAN. You'll be telling me next I'm going to suffer hallucinations.

IRENE. Gillian, there's nothing to keep you here. It's high time you started to take it easy.

GILLIAN. You mean I can stop laying all those golden eggs you're always referring to?

IRENE. Especially if you're not well.

GILLIAN. Not well? Who said I wasn't well?

SPENCE. I did.

GILLIAN. There is nothing wrong with me. I admit I'm a bit tired, but there is nothing else.

SPENCE. Very well. If you say so. I'm only your doctor. Though, if there's nothing wrong with you, I'd like to know why your medicine chest looks like a dispensary.

GILLIAN. Because everyone around me is determined to turn me into a hypochondriac.

IRENE. Why don't you go big-game hunting or something?

GILLIAN. That is supposed to be taking it easy?

IRENE. Climb the Himalayas, then.

(GILLIAN *stares wide-eyed at Irene*)

You can contemplate your navel and gain inner peace.

GILLIAN. I could contemplate my navel right here, but I doubt whether it would give me inner peace. You're not trying to get rid of me, by any chance.

IRENE. Perish the thought. I'm only thinking of you.

GILLIAN. Well, don't.

IRENE. In fact, I was going to offer to stay the night just to make sure you're all right. Would you like that?

GILLIAN. No, I would not. Anyway, as Madge seems to have cancelled her arrangements, she'll be here.

MADGE. I didn't cancel anything, unfortunately. They were cancelled for me.

GILLIAN. I take it that remark means you don't like being here.

MADGE. I didn't say that.

GILLIAN. But you implied it. Well, if you don't like it, then go, girl, go. Well? What're you waiting for?

(*There is an embarrassed pause*)

SPENCE. Gillian, this is doing you no good at all.

IRENE. We know how you feel, but . . .

GILLIAN. Look, in heaven's name! Why is everyone being so solicitous? There was a little accident which upset me. It would have upset anyone. I am now better. Will everyone kindly go home? Good night!

IRENE. You know what you are, Gillian Howard, don't you?
GILLIAN. Whatever I am I've learned to live with it—and like it.

(IRENE *moves up* LC)

SPENCE. Very well. Madge, fetch me that bottle of brandy, will
you?

(MADGE *turns a startled look on the doctor*)

GILLIAN. What?
SPENCE. I'm taking it with me—putting it out of temptation's
way.

(MADGE *exits to the kitchen*)

GILLIAN. What about the Scotch? And the Gin? And the Rose's
lime juice?
SPENCE. You loathe gin and you're not all that fond of Scotch. If
I take the brandy, at least it will mitigate the chances of your killing
yourself, provided you go easy on the lime juice.
GILLIAN (*rising and moving to Spence*) You wouldn't, by any chance,
like to search the flat to see if there's any methylated spirits hidden
away?
SPENCE (*moving down* L) I don't think that will be necessary.

(MADGE *enters with the brandy bottle, which she hands to Spence, looking rather upset by the whole procedure.* SPENCE *looks at the bottle*)

(*to Gillian, moving* C) You've had quite a go at killing this off, haven't
you?
GILLIAN. I have not had a single drink out of that bottle today.
SPENCE. Oh?
IRENE (*moving down* LC *and holding up her hand*) Mea culpa.

(SPENCE *turns to look at Irene*)

No, honestly. You needn't look at me like that. I'm not being all
jolly hockey sticks and standing by my chum. I've been swigging
back that stuff like lemonade.
SPENCE. Since when?
IRENE. Since the accid . . . What the hell has it got to do with
you, anyway?

(SPENCE *shrugs, moves to the hall chair, where she has left her bag, and
puts the bottle away*)

GILLIAN. Are you and my brandy leaving now, then?
SPENCE (*moving up* C) Yes.
GILLIAN. Perhaps you'd like to take Irene with you and drop her
off somewhere.
SPENCE. Of course. (*She looks at her watch*) I would just like to use
your bathroom first, if I may.
GILLIAN. Be my guest.

(SPENCE *goes out up* RC)

What a night! (*She sits on the couch*)
    IRENE. It's all grist to the mill, darling. You'll be able to use it in
one of your books. If you haven't done so already. You can write
another thriller of the year for next year.
    GILLIAN. I could. I could also change my publisher.

(IRENE *moves up* LC. GILLIAN *notices Irene's reaction with satisfaction,
then turns to Madge*)

Madge, phone the travel agency first thing in the morning.
    IRENE. Decided to take my advice for once?

(MADGE *moves* C)

    GILLIAN. And book me a flight to—where? Where would be a
nice place to go? Give me some more of your invaluable advice.

(IRENE *moves down* LC)

    IRENE. What about Italy? Lots of dark, handsome men in Italy.
    GILLIAN. What a splendid idea. You do come up with them some-
times, Irene, don't you? Book me a flight to Rome. I've always loved
Rome.
    IRENE. All roads lead there, so they do say.
    GILLIAN. "All Roads To Rome." Hmn. I think that will be the
title of my next book.
    IRENE. It's probably been used, nearly everything has, includ-
ing . . .
    GILLIAN. Yes, Irene? Including?
    IRENE. You're pushing your luck too far, Gillian.
    GILLIAN. But, darling, it was your suggestion.

(*The front doorbell rings*)

Now, who on earth!

(MADGE *starts to move to the front door*)

Madge! Leave it. (*She rises and moves to the fire*) Perhaps they'll go
away.

(MADGE *stops. They wait. The doorbell rings again*)

    IRENE. Maybe it's the gas board.

(GILLIAN *gives her a withering look. The bell rings again, followed by a
knocking and then a woman's voice*)

    EDITH (*off*) Madge! Madge, are you there?
    GILLIAN. Oh, God! My mother-in-law. Let her in, Madge, or
she'll be standing out there ringing all night. Why couldn't she phone
like any decent, normal, human being?

(MADGE *goes to open the front door*)

IRENE. Because we've been having fun and games with the phone, that's why.

(EDITH *enters up* R *and rushes down* C *to below the couch.* MADGE *moves above the couch*)

EDITH. Gillian! Oh, my poor Gillian! What are you doing?
GILLIAN. Standing by the fireplace.
EDITH. Shouldn't you be in bed?
GILLIAN. If I should be in bed, I would be in bed. Now, what's brought you around, Edith?
EDITH. I tried to call you, but there must be something wrong with your phone. (*She lifts the receiver up and puts it down again*) I heard about your accident.
GILLIAN. From who?
EDITH. Petra. She called me.

(GILLIAN *looks at the others*)

IRENE. She phoned while you were prostrate. She wanted to congratulate you.
GILLIAN. On my accident?
IRENE. Who knows?
EDITH. Are you all right?
GILLIAN. Thank you, darling, I'm fine.
EDITH. What did Doctor Spence say?
GILLIAN. She's in the bathroom—why don't you ask her? It was very good of you to call, Edith, but, now that you've satisfied yourself as to my state of health, you can go away again, can't you? You shouldn't have come out on a night like this in the first place. Remember you are a grandmother.
EDITH. How could I possibly not come around?
GILLIAN. Oh, Edith!
EDITH. You might have been killed! (*She sits on the couch*)
GILLIAN. You would have been duly notified. Now look—all this concern for my well-being and safety—I can't bear it. Your tender affection touches me deeply, but it is all quite unnecessary, so why don't you go home? (*To Irene*) Why don't you go home? And, Madge, why don't you go to bed?
EDITH. What about you?
GILLIAN. I shall be quite all right if I am left alone. You're all quite determined to drive me screaming around the bend. Sitting there clucking like a lot of broody hens.
EDITH. Hadn't one of us better stay with her?
GILLIAN. Madge lives here, remember? She is quite enough. Madge, go to Doctor Spence's bag, get the bottle of brandy, and pour me a good, stiff drink.
MADGE. Oh, no! No, really, Mrs Howard, you can't. You . . .

GILLIAN. Madge, kindly do as I ask or I will not only change my publisher I will also change my secretary.

EDITH. Change your publisher? What are you talking about?

IRENE. It's her idea of a joke.

GILLIAN. No joke, I assure you, no joke. The next book goes to someone else. And don't tell me you didn't have wind of it. (*Yelling*) Madge!

MADGE. Mrs Howard, I wish to hand in my resignation.

GILLIAN. Good. Just pass me the brandy before you go.

(MADGE *goes to the hall for the bottle*)

I'm fast coming to the conclusion that I dislike people intensely. I dislike people on tube trains—

IRENE. When last did you take a tube?

GILLIAN.—and I dislike people in my living-room. I am going to live the life of a recluse.

(IRENE *laughs*)

What are you braying at?

(MADGE *moves above the couch and pours a drink*)

IRENE. You've changed in many ways, Gillian, since Conrad and I published your first book and you stopped riding on tube trains. But in one respect you certainly haven't changed and that's in your need for people of the opposite sex.

GILLIAN. And how am I supposed to have changed?

IRENE. Power corrupts, absolute power corrupts absolutely. The power your money has given you has corrupted you.

GILLIAN. That's nice. That is charming. Now, for the last time, why don't you all go home and leave me to wallow in my own gorgeous, beastly corruption. I enjoy it.

(MADGE *hands Gillian her drink*)

Cheers!

(GILLIAN *lifts the glass, but, before it reaches her lips,* IRENE *suddenly starts to gasp*)

What's the matter with you?

(EDITH *rises.* MADGE *runs up to the hall*)

IRENE (*holding her ribs*) Can't breathe—can't—can't—breathe . . .

MADGE. Doctor Spence! Doctor Spence! Come quickly!

(EDITH *runs* L *to Irene.* IRENE, *her face distorted, crosses below Edith to up* C, *clawing at her chest, trying desperately to get some air into her lungs. Her body jerks forward convulsively as the thorax contracts.* SPENCE *enters from the bedroom and runs to Irene*)

SPENCE. Madge! Help me. My bag!

(MADGE *picks up the bag.* MADGE *and* SPENCE *grab the writhing* IRENE *and, struggling with her, exit to the bedroom.* GILLIAN *and* EDITH *stare at the bedroom door, then* EDITH *turns to Gillian*)

EDITH. How awful! Poor Irene. Whatever's wrong, do you think, Gillian?

(GILLIAN *shakes herself from the stupor into which she seems to have fallen and focuses on Edith*)

GILLIAN. What.
EDITH. I said, what do you suppose is wrong with Irene?
GILLIAN. How should I know?
EDITH. It's lucky Doctor Spence was here.
GILLIAN. Lucky? (*She turns and looks out front and once again raises her glass. She stops, holds the glass in front of her and stares at it with mounting horror before she whispers*) No. No, it's not—possible. It can't be!
EDITH. What?
GILLIAN. Irene—she's been poisoned.

CURTAIN

ACT II

When the CURTAIN *rises,* GILLIAN *is discovered pacing up and down* C. *She stops at the table above the couch and lights a cigarette with quick, nervous movements.* EDITH *enters* L *with a glass of milk and moves up* C *towards the bedroom.*

GILLIAN. You enjoy playing at Florence Nightingale, don't you?

(EDITH *stops by Gillian and places a hand on her shoulder*)

EDITH. Don't worry about Madge, dear. I'm sure she didn't mean it. I'll have a word with her. (*She sails on towards the bedroom*)
GILLIAN. Edith.

(EDITH *stops and turns*)

I'd prefer it if you minded your own business.
EDITH. Gillian—why won't you let people help you?
GILLIAN. Interfering is not helping.

(EDITH *looks hurt*)

(*Moving to the fire*) Oh, Edith—not the mortally wounded look! I can't bear it.

(MADGE *enters from the bedroom*)

MADGE. Have you got . . .

(*Seeing the glass* MADGE *puts out her hand for it, but* EDITH *brushes her aside and, her head held high, marches into the bedroom with the glass.* MADGE *is about to follow her when* GILLIAN *calls*)

GILLIAN. Madge.

(MADGE *stops and turns back*)

Would it help if I apologized?
MADGE (*quietly*) No.
GILLIAN. You've made up your mind. It seems a pity, doesn't it? After all these years? Why, Madge? So suddenly.
MADGE (*moving down* C) It's not sudden, Mrs Howard. I've been thinking of it for some time.
GILLIAN. I thought you were fond of me. (*Silence*) Well, tell me, Madge. Give me reasons. (*Silence*) There must be reasons. (*Silence*) Do you resent me so much you can't even talk about it? (*Silence*) I could never have done it all without you, Madge, you know that.

MADGE. I know it. You know it. Nobody else knows it.

GILLIAN. Who else should know it? It's got nothing to do with anybody else.

MADGE. Hasn't it? What about "The Lady is Dead"?

GILLIAN. What about it?

MADGE. Credit where credit is due, Mrs Howard.

(*It takes a moment for this to sink in and then* GILLIAN *almost laughs*)

GILLIAN. You're not suggesting . . . Oh, Madge!

MADGE. The credit, the success, and all the trappings, you get them all. But that's the way things go, isn't it? You have the name, the reputation.

GILLIAN. And there is absolutely no reason why I shouldn't.

MADGE. You know how much work I did on that book, Mrs Howard.

GILLIAN. Yes, I do. You came up with some ideas, good ones, I won't deny it—and you typed the manuscript.

MADGE. Then there's no more to say, is there? (*She turns up* RC)

GILLIAN. Madge!

(MADGE *exits into the bedroom*)

Madge! (*She runs a hand through her hair and looks around the room. She sees the book, picks it up and looks at it, drops it again. She looks across at the fireplace, then towards the kitchen, then towards the bedroom door*) Three? In one night?

(EDITH *enters up* RC *with the empty glass*)

EDITH. At the rate we're going through the milk, Gillian, you ought to keep a cow in your kitchen.

GILLIAN. Was the operation a success?

EDITH (*putting the glass on the table above the couch*) Oh, I think she's very much better.

GILLIAN. All due to you, no doubt.

EDITH. Madge and the doctor are going to take her home.

GILLIAN. Madge? Why Madge?

EDITH. Because I'm staying here with you.

GILLIAN. Oh, no, you're not!

EDITH. Yes, I am. And I won't have any argument.

GILLIAN. You'll get more than an argument.

EDITH. But my place is here with you.

GILLIAN. Your place is at home in bed. (*She marches to the hall to get Edith's coat and brings it back into the room*) Come on, get into this. When they go, you go.

EDITH. Gillian, do be sensible.

GILLIAN. That's what I am being. Come on.

EDITH. You're in no fit state to be left on your own.

GILLIAN. And you won't be in a fit state for anything if you don't go.

(GILLIAN *stands impotently holding the coat, then she flings it over the back of the couch, picks up the phone and dials. We hear the ringing at the other end.* GILLIAN *taps her foot impatiently*)

EDITH. What are you doing? (*She waits then picks up the glass*) Well, I'll just take this to the kitchen.

(GILLIAN *points imperiously towards the couch*)

GILLIAN. Stay right where you are.

(EDITH *subsides, moves below the couch and sits*)

EDITH (*after a moment*) Gillian?
GILLIAN. Why doesn't he answer?
EDITH. Who are you calling?
GILLIAN. Your great big booby of a son.
EDITH. Martin!
GILLIAN. Yes, Martin.
EDITH. What for?
GILLIAN. To get him to come over here and drag you away, by the scruff of your neck in necessary. (*At the receiver*) Answer, answer.
EDITH. He's probably asleep.

(GILLIAN *gives her a sidelong look*)

Maybe he's gone away for the week-end.
GILLIAN. Mother, ever since we separated you have been on and on trying to get me to talk to Martin. Now that I actually want to, you're not so keen all of a sudden.
EDITH. No—it's not that. (*Rising*) Oh, Gillian, put the phone down. It's obvious he's not going to answer. Well, I'll just pop in and see how they're getting on.

(GILLIAN *stubbornly holds on to the phone as* EDITH *exits into the bedroom. Then, looking around, her eye lights on the bottle of brandy on the table above the couch. She puts down the phone, picks up the bottle, and looks at it, moving slowly up towards the desk. She removes the cork and sniffs it. From her reaction we gather there is so far nothing suspicious. She puts a finger to the mouth of the bottle, tilts the bottle and tastes her finger. Still nothing.* SPENCE *enters quietly from the bedroom.* GILLIAN *looks at the bottle again, then puts it down on the desk. She turns, to find* SPENCE *watching her*)

SPENCE. Been at it again?
GILLIAN. Another remark like that and I'll change my doctor as well. How is Irene?
SPENCE (*putting her bag on the hall table*) On the way to a full recovery, I'm very relieved to say. When she's a bit further on the way we'll take her home.
GILLIAN. Home? Shouldn't she go into hospital?
SPENCE. I don't think so.

GILLIAN. She looked pretty bad to me.

SPENCE. Looks can be very deceptive.

GILLIAN. What's wrong with her?

SPENCE. I really wouldn't like to say. I couldn't with any certainty at the moment.

GILLIAN. Then shouldn't you send her to a hospital to be thoroughly examined?

SPENCE. No.

GILLIAN. But, Beryl, aren't you taking a terrible risk?

SPENCE. I'm the best judge of that. And, anyway, a doctor is always taking risks. Tomorrow her own doctor can see her. If he feels there is need for exploration, then he can send her to hospital.

GILLIAN. Beryl, surely you must have some idea of what it could be.

SPENCE. Oh, yes. It could be one of a number of things.

GILLIAN. Tell me. I mean, maybe I can do something.

SPENCE. Such as what?

GILLIAN. I don't know. Cable her husband in Rome.

SPENCE. Happily that won't be necessary. Now, Gillian, once we've gone, you will stay off the brandy, won't you?

GILLIAN. Oh, don't worry. I won't touch the brandy.

SPENCE. There's a good girl.

GILLIAN (*crossing below Spence to the fire*) Beryl, one of your ideas— I mean—is it possible that Irene might—well, have taken something, eaten something that—er—disagreed with her?

SPENCE. Gillian, how long have I been your doctor?

GILLIAN. Hmn? I don't know—five, six years?

SPENCE. You know me well and I know you inside out.

GILLIAN. Hardly.

SPENCE. Practically. I have never known you not to speak your mind and you have never known me not to take straight speaking. So come on, out with it.

GILLIAN. Was she poisoned?

(SPENCE *stares at Gillian incredulously for a long moment and then breaks into laughter. After a moment she controls herself*)

SPENCE. I'm sorry.

GILLIAN. I take it that means the whole idea is preposterous.

SPENCE (*moving down* C) No, not preposterous—unlikely, but not preposterous. Strychnine maybe. The symptoms could be strychnine poisoning. Curare even, there's a thought. Though, if it were curare, then you really would have to inform the next of kin. Curare is deadly in infinitesimal amounts and the antidote is hardly something a doctor would carry around as a daily necessity. Interesting, though. Then we must ask ourselves, where would she get it? And, more important, why? Presuming she's not suicidal . . .

GILLIAN. Why do you say that?

SPENCE. Presuming, she's not suicidal, who would want to kill her?

GILLIAN. I really don't know. Look, I'm sorry I opened my big mouth; just forget it. And I wouldn't leave her in there with nurse Edith hovering about or she will be killed—by kindness.

(EDITH *enters from the bedroom*)

EDITH. I think she's ready now, doctor.
GILLIAN. Talk of the devil.

(IRENE, *looking very ill, enters from the bedroom, supported by* MADGE)

(*There is genuine concern in her voice. Gone is the hard, brash exterior*) Irene! You look terrible. Are you—I mean, how do you feel?

(SPENCE *and* EDITH *move to help Irene*)

SPENCE. Come along, Mrs Knight.
GILLIAN (*moving below the couch and to up* C) Beryl, don't you think she should stay here?
SPENCE (*moving to the front door*) Do you want to stay here or go home?
IRENE. Home.

(MADGE *takes Irene's coat from its hook*)

GILLIAN. Irene, are you sure? You . . .
IRENE. Home.
SPENCE. Come on, then. Don't worry, Gillian. I will drive her home and Madge will stay with her.
GILLIAN. Madge. When will you be back?
MADGE. I'll see you in the morning, Mrs Howard.
EDITH (*still squeaking around*) Here—let me . . .
SPENCE. It's all right, Mrs Howard, we can manage, thank you.

(MADGE *puts on her coat, then opens the door.* SPENCE *and* IRENE *exit.* MADGE *follows.* EDITH *closes the door behind them, then moves into the room to* R *of Gillian*)

EDITH. That poor woman—that poor woman! Doesn't she look terrible? I don't care what the doctor says, I say she's at death's door. I doubt if she'll last the ni . . .
GILLIAN (*moving away* LC) Oh, for God's sake, Edith! Stop making a bloody meal of it!
EDITH. I'm sorry. I was only being sympathetic.

(EDITH *looks appealingly at Gillian.* GILLIAN *does not respond*)

Well— (*gathering up her coat*) —if you really want me to go, I might as well go. I only came in the first place because I was worried about you—because I thought I might be of some help. (*Silence*) Well, good night, then, Gillian. Go to bed, dear. Get a good night's sleep. You'll feel much better in the morning. (*She moves to the hall*)
GILLIAN. It's morning now.

EDITH. Then sleep in late. (*She goes to the door*) I only hope there's a cab close by.

GILLIAN. Wait.

(EDITH *turns*)

Don't go.

EDITH. What?

GILLIAN (*moving to Edith*) I want to talk to you. I want someone to talk to. Give me that. (*She takes Edith's coat and hangs it up*) Do you want a drink? Tea? Coffee? Oh, hell! No stove. (*She moves to the fire*)

EDITH (*moving L of the couch*) No, of course not, dear. That's all right, I'm quite all right. What do you want to talk to me about?

GILLIAN. Anything. Not Irene. Talk about Martin.

EDITH. Oh, Gillian—do you think there's a chance of a reconciliation? Do you think . . .

GILLIAN. Sit down, Edith, You're cluttering up the room. Isn't it strange how some women clutter everything up without even trying? Just by being there.

EDITH (*sitting on the couch*) I suppose it's because I'm made that way. You're different: so neat and tidy, and practical. That's because you have a neat, tidy, practical mind.

GILLIAN. Not at the moment it isn't. (*She sits on the pouffe*)

EDITH. No, of course not. Have you heard from Mary?

GILLIAN. Hmn? Yes. I had a letter yesterday.

EDITH. How is she enjoying school?

GILLIAN. She hates it. For which I don't blame her one bit.

EDITH. You're looking forward to her coming home, no doubt.

GILLIAN. No. You are. And this time, remember, spots on a boy are bad enough, on a girl they're disaster. Don't spoil her so much. Why don't you get yourself a cat?

EDITH. They bring me out in a rash. I'm allergic to them.

GILLIAN (*suddenly interested*) I never knew that.

EDITH. Anyway, why aren't you looking forward to seeing her? She is your daughter.

GILLIAN. I'm sure she'd much prefer to stay with her father.

EDITH. Did you know he'd been promoted?

GILLIAN. From what?

(*The doorbell rings*)

(*Rising*) Now who is this? Am I keeping open house or something tonight? (*She moves up R of the couch*)

(*The bell rings again*)

EDITH. It could be Martin.

(GILLIAN *stops and turns to look at Edith*)

(*Rising and moving round L of the couch to up C*) Maybe that's why he didn't answer the phone. He was on his way over here. Yes, Petra must have told him.

(GILLIAN *goes to the front door and opens it.* SPENCE *is standing outside*)

GILLIAN. What's the matter?

SPENCE (*crossing below Gillian*) Sorry. Forgot my bag. I must be tired. (*She marches to the hall table, and picks up her bag*)

EDITH. How is Mrs Knight?

SPENCE. Not like me to forget things.

EDITH. We thought it might be Gillian's husband.

SPENCE. What?

EDITH. At the door.

SPENCE. Oh, did you? And a— (*She looks around, obviously not knowing what to say*) —why did you think . . .

EDITH. We were just talking about him and . . .

GILLIAN. Mother, I am quite sure Doctor Spence has far better things to do with her valuable time than stand here gossiping with you about my ex-husband.

EDITH. Not ex, dear, not ex.

GILLIAN. Virtually.

EDITH. And if there's any hope of a reconciliation . . .

SPENCE. Is there?

(GILLIAN *looks at her*)

Hope for a reconciliation.

GILLIAN. No. (*She moves away to the fire*)

EDITH (*moving down* C) But, Gillian! You said . . .

GILLIAN. I didn't say anything.

EDITH. Pardon me, but you did. You said you . . .

GILLIAN. Edith! Will you please mind your own business?

EDITH. Why don't you try calling him again, dear? He might be in now. Maybe he's been out visiting or doing the town and . . .

GILLIAN. Edith!

SPENCE (*looking from one to the other*) Well, I mustn't keep them waiting. Can I give you a lift?

EDITH. No, thank you. I'm staying.

GILLIAN (*moving up to the door; disgustedly*) Doing the town, huh!

SPENCE. Sorry about this. (*She taps the bag*) Good night again.

EDITH. Good night, Doctor Spence. Thank you.

(SPENCE *goes out*)

I think she is such a charming woman. And obviously so reliable.

GILLIAN (*closing the door and moving above the couch*) What did you have to mention Martin for?

EDITH. I don't know, dear, it just came into my head. Did I do wrong?

GILLIAN. No, I don't suppose so. It's just that she knows us both so well, and one doesn't want to wash one's dirty linen in public.

EDITH. Don't be so silly. What's so scandalous about a couple having a tiff? All married couples have tiffs.

GILLIAN. I would hardly call this a tiff. It is a yawning chasm, with Martin on one side and me on the other. Get it into your head, mother, that nothing will bring us together. Nothing.

EDITH. I would have thought Mary might . . .

GILLIAN. Edith!

EDITH. Well, the children do have to be thought about.

(GILLIAN *takes a cigarette from the box and taps it angrily on the table*)

Why don't you divorce him, then?

(GILLIAN *looks at her for a second and then turns away and moves to the fire*)

Well? Why don't you, Gillian? It's obviously the right, I would say, the only thing to do. Can you?

GILLIAN. Can I? Can I what?

EDITH. Divorce him.

GILLIAN. Of course I can.

EDITH (*sitting in the armchair* C) I wonder. Maybe once you've got hold of something as your very own you find it impossible to let go. That's the trouble with collectors, especially collectors of human beings. Do you think that's the fascination in head-hunting?

GILLIAN. Who is interested in head-hunting?

EDITH. Head-hunters, I suppose.

GILLIAN. And you liken me to a head-hunter, do you?

EDITH. Do you know you can buy artificial shrunken heads in novelty shops?

GILLIAN. Really? How interesting. (*She sits* R *on the couch*)

EDITH. Fancy having a whole wall hung with shrunken heads.

GILLIAN. I don't.

EDITH. What do you suppose a head-hunter thinks about when he squats down in his hut and looks at his wall? Do you think it ever occurs to him that his own head might some day end up on somebody's wall?

GILLIAN. I doubt it. Most probably, like a murderer, he doesn't stop to think of the possible consequences of his little game. Now can we talk about something else?

EDITH. Of course, you know all about murder and murderers, being a thriller writer, I mean, having gone into it all so thoroughly. Have you ever committed the perfect murder? In one of your books?

GILLIAN. Why don't you read them and find out?

EDITH. No, I'm not really fond of thrillers.

GILLIAN. To be quite honest, neither am I.

EDITH. I don't like crime being glamorized, you see. I think anti-social behaviour is sordid, dirty. And the most sordid crime of all is murder.

GILLIAN. We are the great moralist tonight, aren't we?

EDITH. Though, I suppose, in some cases, it might be said to be justified.

(GILLIAN *stares at her mother-in-law*)

GILLIAN. You're not serious.

EDITH. Do you really suppose Irene could have been poisoned?

GILLIAN. No.

EDITH. The police are always going on about motives, aren't they? I suppose, if we really look deep enough, at some single point in their lives, anyone could have a motive for killing absolutely anyone.

GILLIAN. What are you suggesting?

EDITH. Nothing. I'm just thinking.

GILLIAN (*rising and moving to the fire*) Your tiny head was never built for thinking, Edith. I don't like this conversation. Head-hunters. Murder. Shall we get back to Martin?

EDITH. What's the point? If there is no chance of a reconciliation and you're not going to divorce him . . .

GILLIAN. Oh, but I am.

EDITH. What?

GILLIAN. Yes. You have just made up my mind for me.

EDITH. But . . .

GILLIAN. Yes, I know. In spite of your saying it's the best thing to do, it's not what you wanted at all, is it?

EDITH. What is it to me?

GILLIAN. I'll tell you what it is to you. It must have come as quite a shock to find your precious son could really be interested in a woman other than his mother. Do you hate me for that? If it hadn't been me it would have been someone else. But, while he is still married to me, and while I have made no will, should anything happen to me, Martin will get everything, no? And everything happens to be quite a lot.

EDITH. Gillian, stop getting so excited.

GILLIAN. Quite a lot. Isn't it? If you've been going through the accounts with Petra you'll know just how much money I have made in the last ten years.

EDITH. Gillian! That remark was offensive.

GILLIAN. Grubbing for money, someone else's money, is offensive.

EDITH. Mary's future does have to be considered.

GILLIAN. Mary will be adequately provided for. (*She suddenly sways and puts her hand to her head*)

EDITH. Gillian! Are you all right?

GILLIAN. Yes—yes—I'm just a bit tired, that's all. (*She suddenly notices the book and looks at it for a moment, then back to Edith*) Edith, why did you ask me about Irene and poison?

EDITH. You were the one who said she'd been poisoned.

GILLIAN (*picking up the book*) In what circumstances would you say murder is justified? Now, that is something you said to me, not I to you. Come on, in what circumstances?

EDITH. I don't know, dear. I was just talking. What are you getting at?

GILLIAN. Edith—someone is trying to kill me.

EDITH (*after a moment; laughing*) Oh, Gillian, I've never heard such nonsense.

GILLIAN. Is it? Is it?

EDITH. Of course it is. Why should anyone want to kill you?

GILLIAN (*softly*) Why should you want to kill me?

(EDITH, *flabbergasted, stares at Gillian*)

For the reasons I've just given you?

EDITH (*rising*) You can't seriously believe . . . This is ridiculous!

GILLIAN. Somebody sent me this today, a copy of my own book. Why?

EDITH. Sent it to you?

GILLIAN. Yes. Sounds absurd, doesn't it? No accompanying letter—nothing—just the book. Explain it.

EDITH. You're the thriller writer, you explain it.

GILLIAN. I've already had that thrown at me once tonight. I don't find it funny.

EDITH. Hadn't you better call the police? Well, go on. If you seriously think someone is trying to kill you, call the police.

GILLIAN. What can they do?

EDITH. They could give you protection. Mount a guard on your door or something.

GILLIAN. What would I say to them?

EDITH (*moving below the couch*) You can tell them how the gas stove blew up on you. It must have been tampered with. How a woman was taken seriously ill in your flat shortly afterwards and you suspect she was poisoned. That you're afraid someone is trying to kill you.

GILLIAN. What a fool they'd think me.

EDITH. No more of a fool than when the coroner brings in a verdict of murder by person or persons unknown.

GILLIAN. You're enjoying this, aren't you?

EDITH. I merely think you are being very silly. (*She moves up* C) Why don't you take a sleeping pill, go to bed, and forget all this ridiculous nonsense?

GILLIAN (*crossing below the couch to down* L) You're trying to lull me into a false sense of security.

EDITH (*moving above the couch*) And you're working yourself into a state of hysteria. Take a walk, then. Some fresh air might help to clear your head.

GILLIAN (*moving behind the desk up* L) No! I am not stepping foot outside this flat. How do I know that isn't exactly what is wanted of me? How do I know someone isn't waiting for me out there? (*She peeps out from behind the curtains and looks down into the street*)

EDITH. You don't know anything. And stop behaving like a cheap character in one of your novels.

GILLIAN (*moving up* C *to* L *of Edith*) Having never read one of my novels, how would you know how one of my characters would behave?

EDITH. I know how you're behaving at the moment and that's . . . Gillian? What's the matter?

GILLIAN (*holding up the book and thinking for a moment*) One of the characters in my books? Wait . . . wait . . . behave like a character—behaviour—characters. Mother, you said a second ago. "I know how you're behaving." Now, if you know how I behave, then others know how I behave, or how they think I will behave in certain circumstances. So what if they deliberately planted those circumstances to make me react? Got it! Not behaviour. Method. Someone is trying to kill me and, whoever it is, is going to use a method I have written about. Yes, that's it. And it's here—its all here—in this book.

EDITH. You really do have a writer's mind, dear. You see fiction in everything.

GILLIAN. Oh, no—this is not fiction. This is fact. But why send me the book? It seems to defeat the whole purpose. Oh, God, I need a drink. (*She goes over to the desk and lifts the brandy bottle, immediately putting it down again with a crash*) Cat and mouse. I am going to kill you, ha ha! Guess how. (*Turning back to Edith*) In this book, Edith, a number of characters are killed and various methods used. One is poisoning, one is electrocution, another is by a gas stove blowing up.

EDITH. You really shouldn't think up such bizarre ways of killing people off. Why don't you do it more humanely?

GILLIAN. It all adds up, doesn't it? Who would want to kill me? You said, anyone at any time could have a motive. It could be you—Irene . . .

EDITH. Oh? Why Irene?

GILLIAN. Because— no, not Irene, because Irene took the brandy that was meant for me. Who then? Martin? Petra? Someone who knows me well.

EDITH. Gillian, you're frightening me. (*Moving towards Gillian*) Look, why don't you come and stay the night with me? You'll be all right with me.

GILLIAN (*moving away down* L) Will I?

EDITH. You don't still think . . . Oh, very well, stay here. Do what you like. I've had quite enough of all this nonsense. I'll telephone in the morning when you've come to your senses. (*She moves up* R)

GILLIAN. I might be dead in the morning.

EDITH. I'll telephone anyway.

GILLIAN (*moving up* C) Edith, Edith, you're not taking me seriously. Or do you still think it's all highly coincidental? And that I'm imagining the rest.

EDITH. I don't know what to think.

GILLIAN. Then think about this; whoever it is obviously thought I would be coming home alone tonight. Whoever it is has access to this flat, came in while I was being fêted and feasted—talk about the fatted calf!

EDITH. Don't go all poetical. That would be fatal.

GILLIAN. Fixed the electric fire, the stove, the brandy—the book could have been left here, the postage faked. But why the book? Yes! That's it! None of these things was meant to kill me, only to frighten. Then I would see the book put two and two together, panic, run out of the flat and . . . (*She brings her hand down on the book with a slap*)

EDITH (*Jumping*) Oh! Oh, don't do things like that.

GILLIAN (*moving to the desk*) So I mustn't leave the flat. I am right. (*She puts the book on the desk*)

EDITH. Are you?

(GILLIAN *turns to look inquiringly at her*)

(*Moving* R *of Gillian*) Have you thought, maybe that's exactly the conclusion they want you to come to? That you would be expected to leave the flat and would deliberately take the opposite course and stay? So, whether you stay here or go out, which is the right thing to do? The answer is you don't know.

(GILLIAN *stares at her*)

How's that for a piece of deduction? Rather clever, I thought. How would you fancy me as a rival?

(GILLIAN *crosses below Edith to up* RC)

GILLIAN. Mother, just turn on that table lamp for me, will you, please? (*She points to the lamp on the table up* R)

(EDITH *crosses below Gillian to the lamp and puts out her hand towards it. Her fingers are practically on the switch when she suddenly realizes. For a moment she stands absolutely motionless, her fingers half an inch from the switch, then turns back to Gillian*)

EDITH. Why did you ask me to switch it on?

GILLIAN (*moving down* C) You haven't switched it on.

EDITH. No. And I'm not going to either.

GILLIAN. Why not?

EDITH. Well er—I . . .

GILLIAN. You're afraid to.

EDITH. Are you surprised? After all the things you've been saying?

(GILLIAN *exits swiftly into the kitchen*)

What are you doing? (*She moves above the couch to* C)

(*We hear a drawer being opened*)

Gillian?

(GILLIAN *enters drawing on a thick rubber glove. She is also carrying a pair of pliers*)

What are you going to do?

GILLIAN (*moving below Edith and above the couch*) Edith, this whole flat is booby-trapped. There is nothing I can touch. (*She approaches the lamp*)

EDITH. You're not going to!

GILLIAN. Right.

(GILLIAN *reaches out determinedly for the lamp switch, but, despite herself, the hand stops. They both strain expectantly towards the lamp.* GILLIAN *tries again. Again she flinches. Finally, head slightly averted, eyes twitching with nerves, she gradually manages to wrap her hand around the lamp and press the switch. The light flicks on. They both heave a sigh of relief*)

EDITH. There—nothing to worry about.

GILLIAN (*moving* c) Edith, I'm right. I know I'm right.

EDITH. That's your trouble, you're always right.

(GILLIAN *glances around the room*)

GILLIAN. Ah! The radio! (*She moves down* L *to the radio and, taking the pliers, switches it on after some hesitation*)

(*There is a bang and a vivid blue flash from the set. The two women shriek and leap back*)

See? See!

EDITH. You don't have to sound so jubilant about it.

GILLIAN (*moving up* RC) All I have to do is keep one step ahead.

EDITH. Where are you going now?

GILLIAN. The electric blanket.

(GILLIAN *exits into the bedroom*)

EDITH. Oh, my God! (*She dithers for a moment not knowing which way to turn*) Is it all right?

GILLIAN (*off*) So far.

EDITH. Oh, why don't you just call the police?

(*No reply comes from the bedroom.* EDITH *dithers a moment longer, then lifts the phone and replaces it, dithering with fear and impotence. There is the sound of bottles clattering in the bedroom*)

What are you doing now?

(GILLIAN *enters with the pliers and a plastic bag full of bottles and jars*)

GILLIAN. From the medicine chest. (*She crosses down* L)

EDITH. Why?

GILLIAN. How do I know they haven't been tampered with? There's no telling what I might be taking. No, the lot goes down the chute.

(GILLIAN *exits into the kitchen*)

EDITH. You'll have to throw all your food away as well.
GILLIAN (*off*) Yes, I will.

(*We hear the bottles rattle away down the garbage chute and then* GILLIAN *returns to the room*)

But that can wait till tomorrow. I hardly feel like eating anything tonight. Now, what next? (*She looks around the room and then at Edith*) You. You're next.

(EDITH *squeaks and backs away up* RC *as* GILLIAN *moves towards her*)

(*Putting the pliers on the table* C) You're not part of the plan, so I think you had better go home. This flat is rather like walking through a minefield and we don't want you blown up, do we?

(GILLIAN *starts ushering* EDITH *towards the hall*)

EDITH. Well, I only hope you know where all the mines are.
GILLIAN. I'll just have to keep my wits about me, won't I?
EDITH. Funny—you playing at detective, after all the ones you've written into your books. It's like a dream.
GILLIAN. As long as we wake up from it.
EDITH. You're being very stubborn, Gillian. I won't say brave . . .
GILLIAN. No, not brave. (*She picks up Edith's coat*)
EDITH. But very stubborn.
GILLIAN (*putting Edith's coat on her*) If I give in I'll go to pieces. Go on now, off with you.

(EDITH *is about to open the front door*)

Wait. (*She puts her hand on the doorknob, slowly opens the door, and peeps out, looking up and down the passage*) All right.
EDITH. I feel like a James Bond heroine.
GILLIAN. You don't look like one.

(EDITH *exits, but returns immediately*)

EDITH. Call the police, Gillian, please!
GILLIAN. Good night, Edith.

(EDITH *exits.* GILLIAN *shuts the door and leans against it. She moves away, then goes back to check the lock. Having satisfied herself, she moves into the room*)

James Bond—tch! (*She moves down* C *to the telephone*) Why doesn't Conrad phone? (*She glances at her watch*) Phone me, Conrad, please! (*She goes to the desk and picks up her reading-glasses and the book. Still looking at the book, she reaches out for the switch of the desk lamp. It is not until her hand is actually on the lamp that she remembers, and jumps back as though scalded, dropping the book to the floor and holding her hand to her heart*) Oh God! That's what they want. (*Looking round the room*) The moments when I forget. The book. (*She picks the book up and starts to flick through it*) It's here—the answer is in here—it must be. Got to be! (*She lowers the book and looks round the room*) Why hasn't he phoned? Why? Keep calm—keep calm. (*She sits in the armchair* C, *opens the book again, and immediately becomes engrossed in it*)

(*There is absolute silence for a few seconds until, suddenly, the telephone rings shrilly.* GILLIAN *gives a little shriek, recovers, and grabs eagerly for the receiver*)

(*Into the receiver*) Yes? (*Silence*) Hello! (*Silence. She starts to panic*) Who is it?

(MARTIN'S *voice is heard on the telephone*)

MARTIN (*on the phone*) Gill?
GILLIAN. Yes?
MARTIN. It's Martin.
GILLIAN. Martin! (*She puts the book on the table*)
MARTIN. Did you try to phone me a short while ago?
GILLIAN. Why should I?
MARTIN. I don't know. I was in the bath when the phone rang . .
GILLIAN. The bath! I forgot the bath.
MARTIN. What?
GILLIAN. Hey? Oh, nothing. Something I forgot to remember.
MARTIN. Anyway, whoever it was rang off just as I got there. Infuriating. Was it you?
GILLIAN. Should it have been?
MARTIN. No, I was just going through the list of probables and . . .
GILLIAN. Clever Martin. Yes, it was. Are you at home?
MARTIN. Well, of course I'm at home. Where do you think I take my baths? What did you want me for?
GILLIAN. Hey? Oh, your mother was here.
MARTIN. Edith?
GILLIAN. You have more than one mother? I thought, if you hadn't gone to bed, you wouldn't mind coming over and taking her home. It's all right now.
MARTIN. She's left?
GILLIAN. Yes, she's left.
MARTIN. You're on your own, then?
GILLIAN. Well, of course I . . . Yes, I'm on my own, for a couple of minutes. I'm expecting Madge back any minute, though. She should have been here by now.
MARTIN. Where is she?
GILLIAN. Oh, she—went visiting—friends.
MARTIN. What did Edith come over for?
GILLIAN. She was lonely. She wanted a nice, cosy chat with her daughter-in-law.

MARTIN. I see. (*After a pause*) Gillian? (*After a pause*) How are you? How are you keeping?

GILLIAN. All right.

MARTIN. I hear you had a big success tonight. Congratulations.

GILLIAN. Thank you. I'm sorry I interrupted your bath. Good night, Martin.

MARTIN. Gillian!

GILLIAN. I'm tired, Martin. Good night. (*She puts down the phone. waits a moment, then picks it up and dials. The phone rings at the other end. She waits and then puts down the phone*) At home is he? Liar. (*She rises, moves away* LC, *then turns back to look at the phone*) But, if he's not at home, where is he? Edith! She phoned him from downstairs. He knows I'm alone. Madge—yes— (*She goes back to the phone. This time the ringing at the other end is cut off almost at once*)

(MADGE'S *voice is heard on the telephone*)

MADGE (*on the phone*) Yes?

GILLIAN. Madge? It's Gillian.

MADGE. Yes.

GILLIAN. How is Irene?

MADGE. She's fine now. Sleeping. Doctor Spence thinks she will be all right tomorrow apart from a sore stomach.

GILLIAN. Has the doctor told you what it was?

MADGE. I don't think she really knows.

GILLIAN. No. I take it she's left.

MADGE. Yes.

GILLIAN. Are you staying there the night?

MADGE. Yes.

GILLIAN. Is that really necessary? I mean, if Irene is all right and asleep. (*Silence*) Madge, you wouldn't think of hopping in a cab and coming back now.

MADGE. No. I'd better stay here.

GILLIAN. But I'd like you to. I mean—well—please, Madge. Get a taxi and come back here. I don't like being on my own, not tonight.

MADGE. There's nothing wrong, is there?

GILLIAN. Well—no—it's just that I feel I need you.

MADGE. If I had been away for the week-end you would have been on your own.

GILLIAN. Yes, but I'm not away and I want you here.

MADGE. No, I'm sorry, Mrs Howard. I really think I should stay here.

GILLIAN. Madge! Please!

MADGE. You will be all right. Good night.

(*The phone clicks down*)

GILLIAN. Madge! (*She rattles the rest*) Madge! Blast! (*She slams down the phone. After a moment she lifts the receiver again. She is trembling and has difficulty in dialling*)

(*The phone rings at the other end and then the receiver is lifted.*
SPENCE's *voice is heard on the telephone*)

SPENCE (*on the phone*) Doctor Spence.
GILLIAN. Beryl—it's Gillian.
SPENCE. What's the matter?
GILLIAN. Can you come over, please? Now? At once.
SPENCE. What's the matter?
GILLIAN. I'm afraid.
SPENCE. Afraid?
GILLIAN. Beryl, I was right. Irene was poisoned. They meant it
for me.
SPENCE. Gillian, you're overwrought.
GILLIAN. Yes, I am! I am! Beryl, please—you've got to come
over. I need someome here with me. Please
SPENCE. But what if I'm needed in an emergency?
GILLIAN. What the hell do you think this is? I tell you someone
is trying to kill me Can't you understand? I don't want to be alone.
Please. Look, do your recorded message thing; use this number. If
anyone wants you they can ring here.
SPENCE. I'm sure if you took a sleeping pill and . . .
GILLIAN. No! No, no, no, no! You've got to come over!
SPENCE (*after a pause*) Well—all right—I'll be over as soon as I
can.
GILLIAN. Hurry!
SPENCE. As soon as I can.

(*The phone clicks off.* GILLIAN *puts down her receiver. She looks around
the room. There is absolute silence. The lights go out and the flat is in
complete darkness.* GILLIAN *gives a little gasp and stands motionless. We
can hear her frightened breathing as suddenly she reaches out for the phone
and, in her haste, knocks it to the floor. She gets down on all fours to retrieve
it. The phone is dead. She rattles the rest. Nothing*)

GILLIAN. Hello! Hello! (*She rattles it again*) Hello! Answer! Oh!
(*She tries dialling, but the phone remains obstinately dead*)

GILLIAN *tenses as she hears footsteps in the corridor outside. They
approach; a slow, measured tread, growing louder until they stop outside her
door. She sits on the floor not daring to move a muscle, and then crumples
into a little heap and starts to whimper as—*

the CURTAIN *falls*

ACT III

Scene—*The same. Twenty minutes later.*

When the Curtain *rises, the flat is still in darkness.* Gillian *is lying on the floor as at the close of the previous Act. The doorbell rings. After a moment it rings again.* Gillian *stirs. The bell rings a third time.* Gillian *rises and goes to the hall. She stands at the front door until the bell rings a fourth time.*

Gillian. Who—who is it?
Spence (*off*) It's me. Beryl. (*After a pause*) Let me in.

(Gillian *opens the door. There is a ray of light from the hall.* Spence *steps inside and* Gillian *slams the door*)

Gillian, what's going on? Have you been sitting here in the dark? Where are the lights? (*She reaches out and gropes for a switch*)
Gillian. It's no good.
Spence. What? (*She finds the switch and flicks it up and down several times*)
Gillian. God, I'm so glad you're here.
Spence (*putting her bag on the table in the hall*) What's wrong with the lights? What are you playing at?
Gillian. They just went out, without any warning.
Spence. So a fuse went. Why didn't you fix it? Not much fun sitting in the dark all on your own, is it? Where's your fuse box?
Gillian. What?
Spence. Your fuse box.
Gillian. No! You mustn't touch it.
Spence. Why not?
Gillian. It's dangerous. You could be hurt.
Spence. Well, of course electricity is dangerous if you monkey about with it without knowing what you're doing, but I can do a simple job like fixing a fuse. Now—where is the box?
Gillian. (*after a pause*) In the kitchen, above the door.
Spence. Thank you. (*She crosses the room to down* l) Where do you keep the fuse wire?
Gillian (*moving down* c) Fuse wire?
Spence. You don't expect me to repair it with a piece of string, do you?
Gillian. Fuse wire . . .
Spence. Never mind. I'll look. Have you got a torch?
Gillian. Torch?

SPENCE. Gillian, stop repeating everything I say. Have you got a torch?

GILLIAN. No.
SPENCE. Candle?

(GILLIAN *shakes her head*)

No candle. All right, I'll see what I can do.

(SPENCE *exits into the kitchen*)

GILLIAN. Maybe the wire is in the drawer.
SPENCE (*off*) Which one?
GILLIAN. In the dresser, on the left.

(*We hear* SPENCE *open a drawer and rummage through it*)

SPENCE (*off*) You really are having a night, aren't you?
GILLIAN. That is the understatement of the year.
SPENCE (*off*) What?
GILLIAN (*loudly*) I said . . .

(SPENCE *enters* L)

SPENCE. The best place to keep fuse wire—this is for future reference when you've bought a torch or a packet of candles—is on top of the box itself. Then you'll never forget where it is.
GILLIAN. That's where it is.
SPENCE. What?
GILLIAN. I forgot.
SPENCE. Isn't it marvellous.

(SPENCE *exits into the kitchen.* GILLIAN, *not being able to resist it, moves over to the kitchen door to watch*)

GILLIAN. Use a stool.

(*The stool is dragged across the kitchen floor*)

Can you find the main switch?
SPENCE (*off*) Bring me your table lighter; I'll use that.

(GILLIAN *gets the lighter and takes it across to the kitchen door.* SPENCE *has climbed up on to the stool, so that we see* GILLIAN *hand her the lighter just inside the door and the flicker of light as she takes out the fuses above the door*)

How long is it since they went?
GILLIAN. Twenty minutes? Thirty? I don't know.
SPENCE. And you've been sitting here doing nothing all this time? This one's gone. Here. (*She passes down a fuse*)

(GILLIAN *takes the fuse*)

And this one. (*She passes down another fuse*)

(GILLIAN *takes the second fuse*)

If the master fuse has gone, God knows where that is, and you've got to call in the Electricity Board to fix it. Give us your hand.

(GILLIAN *puts her hand through the door and helps her off the stool.* SPENCE *enters the room*)

Thanks. Come to think of it, it couldn't have gone or the whole building would be in darkness, and the lights are on outside. Tch! The wire's the wrong amperage.

GILLIAN. How come you know so much about it?

SPENCE. One picks things up. I don't suppose you've got such a thing as pair of pliers?

GILLIAN. Yes. (*She picks them up from the table* c *and hands them to* Spence)

SPENCE. Surprise surprise. (*Moving* c) What are they doing there?

GILLIAN. Oh, I was using them earlier this evening.

SPENCE. What for?

GILLIAN (*moving to the window*) If I open the curtains, you'll be able to work from the street lights. (*She pulls open the curtains and releases the catch on the window*)

SPENCE. What? Four floors up? No, I'll go into the corridor. (*She starts for the front door*) If you really want to do something useful, pour me a drink.

GILLIAN. What?

SPENCE. Scotch. And water, half and half.

GILLIAN. I'll see if I've got any.

SPENCE. You have. Sudden thought. Did you check all the lights?

GILLIAN. No. I didn't think of it.

SPENCE. Well, some of them might be still on, you goof. Tch!

(SPENCE *exits up* RC. GILLIAN *watches and suddenly a shaft of light appears through the door*)

(*off*) See? You might at least have tried.

GILLIAN (*turning down* c) I'll get your drink. (*She notices the phone lying on the floor, the receiver still off. She goes over to it and picks it up, listens to it, jiggles the rest. The phone is still dead. She puts it down on the table*) Thank God it's stopped raining. It's quite pleasant now.

SPENCE (*off*) What?

GILLIAN. I said it's quite pleasant, now the rain's stopped.

SPENCE (*off*) Where's my drink?

GILLIAN. Oh, yes. Coming.

(GILLIAN *exits into the kitchen.* SPENCE *enters from the bedroom, puts the wire and pliers on the desk, and exits into the kitchen. They are both just visible in the doorway as* SPENCE *tries the fuses*)

SPENCE. Here's the first. Give me a hand.

(GILLIAN *helps* SPENCE *up on the stool*)

Which light do you want on first?

GILLIAN. In here, I think.

SPENCE. Right.

(SPENCE *tries a fuse and the lights in the main room come on and go off as she pulls it out*)

Oops! Wrong one.

(*She tries again and the kitchen light comes on*)

There you are. (*She climbs down from the stool and re-enters the room, sits on the desk and, by the light coming from the kitchen, starts work with the wire and the pliers on the remaining fuses*)

(GILLIAN *enters with the drinks tray, takes it over to the table above the couch and picks up the Scotch bottle. She starts to pour. The bottle clinks against the glass. SPENCE looks up to see GILLIAN trembling, says nothing, but goes back to the fuse. GILLIAN takes the glass across to her*)

GILLIAN. Oh, damn! I forgot the water.

SPENCE (*taking the glass and putting it on the desk*) Never mind. I'll get it in a minute.

(GILLIAN *moves away above the couch.* SPENCE *watches her*)

All right, Gillian start at the beginning. Tell me all about it.

GILLIAN (*shaking her head*) What's the point?

SPENCE. The point is, I would like to know. What is wrong? You got me to come over here because you were in a high old state of hysteria and I don't believe a succession of minor mishaps . . .

GILLIAN. You—you call tonight a succession of minor mishaps? Beryl, don't you know why I didn't want to stay here on my own tonight? Can't you guess? Look what has happened since I came home tonight!

SPENCE. If you ask me, the whole flat needs rewiring.

GILLIAN. What about Irene?

SPENCE. Yes, maybe she needs rewiring as well.

GILLIAN (*moving to the fire*) Stop being so flippant.

SPENCE. Well, I can't take it seriously.

GILLIAN. Why not?

SPENCE. Who was the English king who told so many stories about the battles he had led and won that eventually he firmly believed his own stories? When in actual fact he got no nearer a battlefield than the bedchamber.

GILLIAN (*shaking her head*) Edith didn't take me seriously either.

SPENCE. What happened to her? Did you finally persuade her to go home? Maybe you should have persuaded her to stay instead. There—(*She finished the fuses*)—let's get these two in and we're back to normal. (*She rises and moves to the kitchen*)

GILLIAN (*moving below the couch*) Beryl, please listen to me.

SPENCE. Wait till I get the lights back on.

GILLIAN. Don't you believe it's possible someone might be trying to murder me?

SPENCE. I suppose it's possible. Anything is possible. I think it's rather unlikely, that's all. Now, can I put these in?

(SPENCE *climbs up on the stool. There is a moment before the lights come on in the main room and* SPENCE *jumps down again, moving the stool from the doorway*)

There, all done. (*Moving to the desk*) Who needs a man about the house? Now I'll have that drink. (*She picks up her glass and moves down* L *to the kitchen door*)

GILLIAN. Do you know yet what's wrong with Irene?

SPENCE. No. But I left her quite comfortable and, if there's any trouble, Madge will telephone.

GILLIAN. Do you still maintain she couldn't have been poisoned?

SPENCE. As I said, anything is possible.

GILLIAN. But rather unlikely.

(SPENCE *shrugs and exits into the kitchen*)

While you were there, did Madge say anything about me?

SPENCE (*off*) Madge was her usual untalkative self. What should she have said?

GILLIAN. Oh, nothing. (*She shivers and hugs herself, looking around the room*)

(SPENCE *enters and sees this. She moves in to* C)

SPENCE. Cheers. (*She drinks*)

(GILLIAN *watches Spence for a moment*)

GILLIAN. I'll not imagining it, Beryl.

SPENCE. Then why haven't you phoned the police?

GILLIAN. Because I didn't want to make a fool of myself.

SPENCE. But if you think someone is trying to kill you!

GILLIAN. Oh, I don't know. I wish I had done now.

SPENCE. Do you suspect anyone?

GILLIAN. Yes.

(SPENCE *picks up the phone and holds it out to Gillian*)

SPENCE. Phone for the police.

GILLIAN. I can't.

SPENCE. Don't be stubborn, Gillian. Phone for the police.

GILLIAN. I can't! The phone is dead.

SPENCE (*putting her glass on the table* C) What? (*She puts the receiver to her ear, rattles the cradle, then puts down the phone*) That is strange, I mean, on top of everything else, that is strange.

GILLIAN. You're beginning to believe me?

SPENCE. I don't know. But I still can't see who. Or why. Who do you suspect?

GILLIAN. Martin.

SPENCE. Martin?

GILLIAN. I would have said Irene, but I can discount her.

SPENCE. Can you?

GILLIAN. Of course. If it had been her she would have known about the brandy.

SPENCE. Oh, yes. (*Moving to the desk*) The brandy. (*She goes over to the brandy bottle and goes through the same smelling and tasting routine as Gillian did earlier*)

GILLIAN (*moving to the fire*) I've already done that. It tastes and smells like brandy.

SPENCE. Which, considering the label on the bottle, is what it should taste and smell of. I'll get the police, let them sort it out. (*She starts for the hall*)

GILLIAN (*moving up R of the couch*) No, not yet.

SPENCE (*turning up C*) But, Gillian, it's the obvious thing to do.

GILLIAN. No. I don't want to be left alone again.

SPENCE. Well, we can get around that easily enough; come with me.

GILLIAN. No! I don't want to leave this flat. I just want you to stay with me for the rest of the night—what's left of it. I've thought of everything in here that can possibly harm me. I'm safe here. You see it was very carefully planned, but for one thing, and that is I was expected to come home alone. Irene coming in with me was unexpected and so was Madge not being away for the week-end. So the plot has misfired.

SPENCE. Are you sure you thought of everything? You let me fix the fuses knowing they might have been tampered with.

GILLIAN. You insisted.

SPENCE. Yes, but you might have warned me. So you think you're quite safe, sitting here.

GILLIAN. I think so.

SPENCE. You think so. You suspect someone is trying to kill you, you don't know who it is, or why, and you think so. Well, if you're not going to do the sensible thing and go to the police, I'm going to leave you to it.

GILLIAN. No! You can't leave me here alone!

SPENCE. I can and I am. If you don't like it, then you can come home and stay with me.

GILLIAN. Beryl, please!

SPENCE. All right, if you insist upon staying here, I'll give you some of your medicine. You can lock yourself in, go to bed, and wake up in the morning wondering what all the hysteria was about. (*She starts for the bedroom*)

GILLIAN. I haven't got any medicine.

SPENCE. What?

GILLIAN. It's all gone. I threw it away.

SPENCE. Why?

GILLIAN. Because it could have been one of the dangers. Don't you see?

SPENCE. Yes. Well, in that case, I had better give you something. (*She picks up her bag*)

GILLIAN. I am not going to sleep.

SPENCE (*moving above the couch*) I don't care what you do after I've gone, but I have other patients to think of.

GILLIAN. If they find this number out of order they'll dial emergency. You don't have to worry.

SPENCE. But I do. (*She places her bag on the table above the couch and takes from it a hypodermic syringe, cotton wool and bottle*)

GILLIAN. What is it?

SPENCE. It's all right. It won't put you to sleep, merely calm your nerves.

GILLIAN. Please stay. I would rather you just stayed.

SPENCE. No Gillian. (*She prepares and fills the syringe*)

GILLIAN (*moving R of the couch and below it*) I asked Madge to come back but she wouldn't. Beryl, once you've gone, I won't be able to get anyone else. Oh God! What if anything should happen to me? (*She sits R on the couch*)

SPENCE. Nothing is going to happen to you.

GILLIAN. No one would know. I wouldn't be able to get hold of anyone. I would be completely alone.

SPENCE (*moving L of the couch and below it with the syringe, cotton wool and surgical spirit*) And for that you have no one to blame but yourself. Come on now, let's get this over and done with. (*She rub's Gillian's arm with the spirit*)

GILLIAN. Poor Madge, I suppose I did treat her pretty badly.

SPENCE. It's a little late to start thinking of Madge.

(SPENCE *takes up the syringe, and it is almost at* GILLIAN's *arm when suddenly she screams and leaps away, clutching at the arm that nearly felt the needle*)

Gillian!

(*The two women stand facing each other*)

GILLIAN. You!

SPENCE. What?

GILLIAN. No—no, it can't be—but why?

SPENCE. What are you talking about?

GILLIAN. The syringe—the syringe—I forgot the syringe!

SPENCE. Aren't you being very, very silly?

GILLIAN. Am I?

SPENCE. I should have gone when I said I was going. Well, I don't intend to put up with your nonsense any longer, so I will just give you this injection and . . .

GILLIAN. No! And I invited you here, to come and stay with me! Because I didn't want to be on my own. And it was you all the time.

SPENCE. Gillian . . .

GILLIAN. No! Don't come near me! Stay away! Heart failure. You were going to tell them I died of heart failure. That's what you planned, isn't it?

SPENCE. I didn't plan anything and, if you carry on the way you're going, you will have heart failure.

GILLIAN. What's in that syringe?

SPENCE. I told you, something to make you relax.

GILLIAN. And what did you put in the brandy? You're a doctor—it could have been a drug—and when Madge phoned to say I had had an accident and you realized there was someone else in the flat you rushed over realizing that something could go wrong.

SPENCE. I rushed over because I was called to see you.

GILLIAN. And when Irene said she had drunk the brandy which was meant for me you had to act quickly, so instead of just leaving as you were about to do, you said you wanted to use the bathroom. But you didn't go to the bathroom. You stood behind that door and waited for the moment when Irene collapsed. You came belting out of there like a bat out of hell because it really would have been too bad had Irene died in my place.

SPENCE. It's no wonder you're a best-seller. You really do have a vivid imagination. Perhaps a little too vivid for your own good.

GILLIAN. And when I asked you about Irene you were deliberately vague. You had to be.

SPENCE. Gillian, really, this is all . . .

GILLIAN. So what was it you put in the brandy?

SPENCE. In all this theorizing, isn't there something you've forgotten?

GILLIAN. What?

SPENCE. How did I get into your flat while you were out? I don't have a key.

GILLIAN. The porter let you in.

SPENCE. I thought murderers did their best to remain invisible.

GILLIAN (backing to the fire) Then you have an accomplice. Someone you're . . . Madge! Yes, Madge. Why didn't I think of it?

SPENCE (laughing) What? Now, why on earth should I want to join forces with Madge to kill you? Oh, Gillian, can't you see how silly this is? I really should be very angry, but, as you've had a pretty rough night—well, tomorrow you'll wonder how you could have behaved so foolishly. Now . . .

(SPENCE moves forward but, GILLIAN dodges below her and backs away. SPENCE stops)

Gillian, I am going to forget myself and get angry in a minute.

GILLIAN (backing below the L end of the couch) Go away. Get out. Go home. I don't want you here.

Spence (*moving below the couch towards Gillian*) I can't go and leave you in this state.

Gillian. You mean you won't go. (*She backs against the table* c. *The phone starts to fall, but she catches it*) Did you put the phone out of action?

Spence. Gillian, you're determined to believe all this, aren't you?

Gillian. Because I'm right.

Spence. Because you're stubborn, as you have always been stubborn. Because you have taken a stand and won't budge. Because you are always right and you can never see anyone else's point of view. Because you can never think of anything but Gillian Howard. Because, to you, other people do not have lives of their own, only lives that revolve around you.

Gillian. Martin. You and Martin. That's how he knew I had phoned him. He was with you all the time.

Spence. Yes, Gillian. Martin. We want to get married.

Gillian. What's stopping you?

Spence. You are.

Gillian. No, I'm not. I'm giving him his divorce. He'll be free to marry you.

Spence. You're only saying that because you're frightened.

Gillian. No! No, I mean it. I told Edith tonight. I told her! I'm going to divorce him. You've got to believe me!

Spence (*advancing on Gillian*) It's too late, Gillian.

Gillian. No, stay away! (*She backs above the table to up* rc)

Spence. It's too late. You're done for, Gillian. You're dead.

Gillian (*backing above the upstage end of the desk*) But why? Why want to kill me now? I mean, there's no reason now.

Spence (*following Gillian*) Oh, but there is. True, if you give Martin a divorce I can have him, eventually. But, if you die, I can have Martin and your money. It will be the perfect murder, Gillian. I have three witnesses to the state you were in tonight and they know of your heart condition.

Gillian (*backing round the desk towards the window*) What heart condition?

Spence (*following Gillian closely*) The one I told them about. I am, after all, your doctor. I should know.

(Spence *moves forward and* Gillian, *realizing she is up against the open window, screams and runs down* l. Spence *follows her*)

I'm going to get you, Gillian. There seems little point in delaying the inevitable.

Gillian. Beryl—listen to me—please! Please listen!

(Spence *moves forward quickly and* Gillian *is forced to beat a hasty retreat. She stumbles and* Spence *darts in.* Gillian *screams and evades her running below her to up* l)

Beryl! Don't! Don't do it! Listen to me . . . I'll give you what you want. I'll give it to you. (*She grabs the chair below the desk and throws it down between* Spence *and herself*) I'll give you money. You can have Martin, money, anything I can give you.

SPENCE. No. Tonight you will give me the world—but what about tomorrow? Let's call this insurance against tomorrow. I've got to do it now.

GILLIAN. Please! Please!

(*Relentlessly* SPENCE *closes in. Now* GILLIAN *appears petrified, unable to move. She stands staring at* SPENCE *advancing on her. Suddenly the spell is broken.* GILLIAN *turns and runs for the front door.* SPENCE *does not follow as* GILLIAN *struggles for a second with the lock, sobbing with fright, opens the door and runs out into the corridor, leaving the door open.* SPENCE *stands waiting for something. There is a moment's silence and then we hear the sound of a lift gate being closed. There is a terrible scream from* GILLIAN, *then silence*)

SPENCE. She forgot the lift. (*She puts the syringe on the desk, picks up the book from the table* C *and, turning to the very end, starts to read*) "In front of her was the ancient lift, like a huge, ornate birdcage; a once handsome, gilded birdcage, now a dull ugly thing, tired and old. She did not question the cage being on her floor or notice the doors were slightly ajar. She was only a few steps from the safety of the cage. She pulled back the doors, almost flung herself inside, slammed the doors closed. Still clutching the handle of the inner gate she slumped lifeless to the floor of the cage. The man stepped from the shadows and swiftly unhooked the high-voltage wires from the gate." (*She closes the book*) And the doctor, being on hand most conveniently, will now go out and decide on the cause of death—heart failure. (*She puts the book on the table* C, *picks up the syringe, cotton wool and bottle of spirit and packs them in her bag. She looks round the room, then picks up the brandy bottle and puts that also into the bag. She turns to go, moving up* C)

(GILLIAN *appears in the doorway. For a moment the two women stand looking at each other, then* GILLIAN *moves into the room*)

GILLIAN. Isn't it amazing how even the perfect murder can so easily go wrong? Poor Madge. She must have had a change of heart after my call. People are always leaving those lift gates open, and when she had to climb four flights of stairs she couldn't let someone else do the same. She was closing them just as I ran out.

(SPENCE *darts below Gillian towards the front door*)

It's no good. The police are here.

(SPENCE *turns and looks at her*)

It seems as though Edith did take me seriously after all. I should think they're already asking Martin some rather awkward questions. You wouldn't care for a brandy while we wait?

CURTAIN

FURNITURE AND PROPERTY LIST

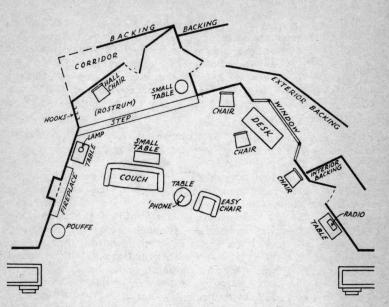

ACT I

On stage: Couch (RC)
Armchair (C)
Pouffe (down R)
Chair (below desk)
Chair (up LC)
Chair (above door down L)
Chair (in hall)
Table (in hall)
Table (above fire) *On it:* lamp
Table (C) *On it:* telephone, ashtray
Table (down L) *On it:* radio
Table (above couch) *On it:* cigarette-box, lighter, ashtray, tray
    with brandy, Scotch, glasses (not on tray)
Desk (up L) *On it:* writing materials, lamp, pile of mail, wrapped
    book, address book, reading glasses
Carpet
Hall rug
Window curtains (open)
On wall in hall: hooks

Off stage   Glass of whisky and water (MADGE)
Glass of whisky and water (MADGE)
Small medical bag *In it:* hypodermic syringe, cotton wool, bottle of spirit, rubber-stoppered bottle

Personal: SPENCE: watch
GILLIAN: watch
MADGE: umbrella

ACT II

Set: Edith's coat on chair in hall

Off stage: Glass of milk (EDITH)
Drawer, to be opened (GILLIAN)
Rubber gloves (GILLIAN)
Pliers (GILLIAN)
Plastic bag of bottles and jars (GILLIAN)

ACT III

Off stage: Stool (SPENCE)
2 fuses (SPENCE)
Fuse wire (SPENCE)
Drinks tray (GILLIAN)

LIGHTING PLOT

Property fittings required: wall brackets, 2 table lamps, electric fire.

INTERIOR: A lounge. The same scene throughout.

THE APPARENT SOURCES OF LIGHT are brackets and lamps.

THE MAIN ACTING AREAS are R, up RC, down RC, C, up LC, LC, down L

ACT I   Night

To open: Light on in corridor off R. Room in darkness

Cue 1   GILLIAN switches on lights   (Page 1)
Snap on brackets

Cue 2   GILLIAN pushes home fire plug   (Page 3)
Bright flash from fire

ACT II   Night

To open: As close of previous Act

Cue 3   GILLIAN switches on lamp R   (Page 33)
Snap on table lamp R

Cue 4   GILLIAN switches on radio   (Page 33)
Blue flash from radio

Cue 5   After GILLIAN replaces telephone receiver   (Page 37)
Snap to Black-out except for corridor light

ACT III   Night

To open: As close of previous Act

Cue 6   SPENCE exits up RC   (Page 40)
Snap on light in room off RC

Cue 7   SPENCE: "Right"   (Page 41)
Snap room lighting on and off

Cue 8   SPENCE: "Wrong one"   (Page 41)
Snap on light in kitchen down L

Cue 9   SPENCE puts in fuses   (Page 42)
Snap on room lighting

EFFECTS PLOT

ACT I

ACT II

ACT III

PRINTED AND BOUND IN GREAT BRITAIN BY
BUTLER & TANNER LTD.,
FROME AND LONDON